artifacts

&

PARALLAX

artifacts & PARALLAX

Stephen J. Van Hook

Glen Park Press
2017

For Jenny, Jacob and Dietre

Thanks to my family & friends for their support & encouragement, especially Jim Colbert, Doug Irwin, Jon Vickers-Jones and Amalia Shaltiel.

Thanks to my many wonderful teachers over the years, especially Betty Lotterman, the high school teacher who first got me to write and who modeled how a good teacher is as committed to helping a student grow as a person as much as to learning the course material.

Finally, a hearty thanks to fellow "Middle-Aged Rock God" Jim Colbert for his striking cover design.

"Plectra Perplexion" and "Bonhoeffer" were previously published in Jon Vickers-Jones' *JVJ with family and a few of his friends* (2017).

First Printing: 2017

ISBN 978-0-9665009-3-6

Glen Park Press
690 Tanager Drive
State College, PA 16803

Introduction

A shard of a cooking pot, an arrowhead, an old letter, an Art Deco building – even a Commodore 64 computer – serves as a physical artifact of our lives. Each artifact provides a window through which we see back in time dimly, a telling yet incomplete picture of a particular moment in human existence. Examining multiple artifacts, each providing a distinct perspective, more fully reveals the depth and complexity present in our world – just as parallax in vision provides us depth perception and so allows us to see our surroundings in all three spatial dimensions.

These poems and song lyrics, written over the last five years, form ink & paper artifacts illustrating varying fragments of life. Some of these artifacts illustrate the serious side of life. Others the silly side. Some reflect the rush of sudden, fully formed inspiration. Others, an arduous crafting over an extended period of time. Some were inspired by my own experiences. Others by world events and the stories of others. And some came from the æther insisting to be told.

Accompanying these artifacts of words are artifacts of images, photographs documenting both human construction and natural formation. See pp. 120-122 for details on each photograph and notes about several of the poems & songs.

I invite you to enjoy these photographic & poetic artifacts, and the parallax of shifting perspective they offer.

Stephen J. Van Hook
Six-string packing poet

June 2017

Table of Contents

Artifacts & Parallax

Artifacts

An archaeological dig
Through the strata of my life,
Each folder, bin, or binder
A mildewy artifact of a
Nearly forgotten past.

Each brings its remnant memory
For a moment to the fore:
Jacob playing ball kicks with Ty in the lobby &
Counting down Metro stops to elephants & rockets,
Dietre the unquenchable aspiring artist,
Grinning trickster & designer extraordinaire.
That GPS project with Lane –
Finding a friend and racquetball partner –
Kenwood science lessons,
Singing songs with kindergartners:
Balls of Air,
Lift, Squeeze, Stretch & Twist.
RIPE & PRISM with Tracy
Sound, magnets, machines
Phases of the moon, electricity
Light lessons for 4th graders
Pipe insulation roller coasters.

I brought to Webster's bags of books
From these lifetimes past,
Recycled years of *Black Belt* magazines
& Decades of physics lecture notes.
Unwanted reminders
On needed shelf space.

Found the two novels I attempted in vain
(One finished, one a grab bag of awkward scenes)
And a few incomplete children's books
From back when our kids were *so* young,
And we'd sing together: *Dietre & the Bug*.

Parallax

Switch from left to right
First one eye, then the other –
A different world, a different
    Perspective
To discover.

For what from one angle
Is most clearly true
Is less obvious
    (even false)
From another point of view.

Both one truth & many,
For she says left & right;
But he says right & left
& You see them in line.

The constellations in the sky
A mere accident of location
& Multiple
    Perspectives
Provide depth
Perception.

Illusions of forced perspective
You'll see past with both eyes,
For one view gives mere knowledge
But more can make you wise.

Stereogram images
Cross your eyes just enough that a third image appears in between
one of the pair of photographs taken from slightly different angles.
This middle image will be three-dimensional.

Bradley Beach

So why stroll down the boardwalk to Bradley Beach
To see the house where we stayed six summers ago?
After all, the beaches are indistinguishable
& The houses less impressive
Than those in God's square mile,
Ocean Grove,
A place already soaked
With its own disjoint remembrances
From my childhood decades ago.

Perhaps because back in State College,
All eight years of our unfolding story blend & blur,
While this place forms a distinct fixed point,
Where a single strobe flash illuminates memories
And locks their place in time,
That week but a mere frame in a still-developing film.

Six years ago, Jacob just out of 6th grade, Dietre out of 3rd.
Both shorter than me, then; the opposite now true.
We boogie-boarded for hours; now their interest less keen.
They hole up in their rooms more now,
But still come out for ice cream.
That was before the Folk Show and the Acoustic Brew,
Before songwriting,
Before Jenny as PRI Director,
When State College still felt so very new.

I had forgotten about the mini-golf and playground
          just 'cross the street
Where the younger kids would run 'round when not on the beach.
Though our boys, a bit older,
Were never part of that gang,
Partly excluded,
Partly just doing their own thing.
Though it was harder on Dietre,
Closer in age.

Tai Chi my passion then, I woke early for form on the wet sand
As the fishermen engaged in their own brand
        of morning meditation.
We played Rook in the evenings, read books on the front slab
Needed to get back into shape, but ate through junk food instead.
Had family portraits taken, gave glassblowing a try,
We celebrated our parents' 50th anniversary
A year early, and we wondered why.
("You never know what can happen," Mom ominously had said.)

Aunt Marilyn and Uncle Jerry visited one afternoon,
'Twas to be the last time, but didn't know then
That they would both, sadly, pass on so soon.
Though was clear that day that Jerry was a mere shadow
Of the firmly confident man he had been.

One drizzly dawn Jacob and I walked the beach
      north to Asbury Park
As I shared what it had been like as a kid there 30 years before,
When we'd come here each summer with Poppop & Aunt Marge.
And after hours of wave jumping and sand castle building,
We'd indulge in games & ice cream & salt water taffy.
But it was hard for him to picture it on that gray morning:
With Skee-ball, mini-golf, and carousel long gone,
& Only the hollowed-out shell of the arcade remained.
Though Madame Marie survived ("Oh, Sandy…")
As Bruce long ago might have claimed.

Now, six years later, I walk alone
On the boardwalk to Bradley Beach all on my own
Return to review that celluloid frame,
To see it more clearly from whence it was made.
To revisit a moment when my boys were much younger
When time felt less heavy, and we felt less busy,
When I hadn't yet made these six years of mistakes
& Before to sepia, this master print fades.

This house in Ocean Grove will take its own place
In our flickering home movie, yet another grainy frame,
Still life – flaws and all – of whom we are now,
Snippets and snatches of our family together today:
With Jacob going to college, off to Penn State,
Dietre in high school still finding his way.

On the front porch with Aunt Marge, my parents read & chat,
And occasionally over their books have dozed off for a nap.
A recent fall in Costa Rica has Mom for now hobbled
& Since Bradley Beach, Dad's faced knee replacement troubles.
Thus they unfortunately both struggle
With walking on the sand,
Still Mom joins us in the surf –
We just give her a hand.

I play Tai Chi on the beach as the sun begins to rise,
Then guitar on the pier while a new song I improvise –
Inspired by a young mother having fun trying to show
Her three small children yoga pose after pose
In the sand one gorgeous early morning.
We eat surf tacos, crepes on the boardwalk & ice cream at Nagles,
We see a whale offshore, boogie board & have fun parasailing.

So next time I'm nearby, I'll walk over to this place
To retrieve this moment & keep it, too, from fading away.

Protagonist

I am my own protagonist;
        Yet you are yours, too.
Though I know you are evil,
        For I see what you do.
I, on the other hand,
        Do what's right, or at least
Mean well – mostly –
        In all of my deeds.
I may not be perfect,
        This protagonist flawed,
But there are reasons for my sins,
        As I've explained to God.
However, you, oh cretinous
        Mean S.O.B.,
There's no justification for you,
        Oh how can there be?
Yet in your warped mind,
        I'm the villain & the hero is you.
For even Grendel tells the story
        From his own point of view.

America

America,
>Lighthouses, covered bridges
>White steepled churches
>Fall colors, winter snow
>Revolution graves.

America,
>Land of the free
>& Home of the brave.

America,
>Empire State Building view
>Brooklyn Bridge, 5th Avenue
>Ellis Island immigrants
>Lady Liberty.

America,
>"Send me your huddled masses,
>Yearning to breathe free."

America,
       Rolling hills of feed corn
       Green John Deere caps worn
       Grain elevators rise
       High in the sky.

America,
       Jim Crow, Trail of Tears,
       Massacre at My Lai.

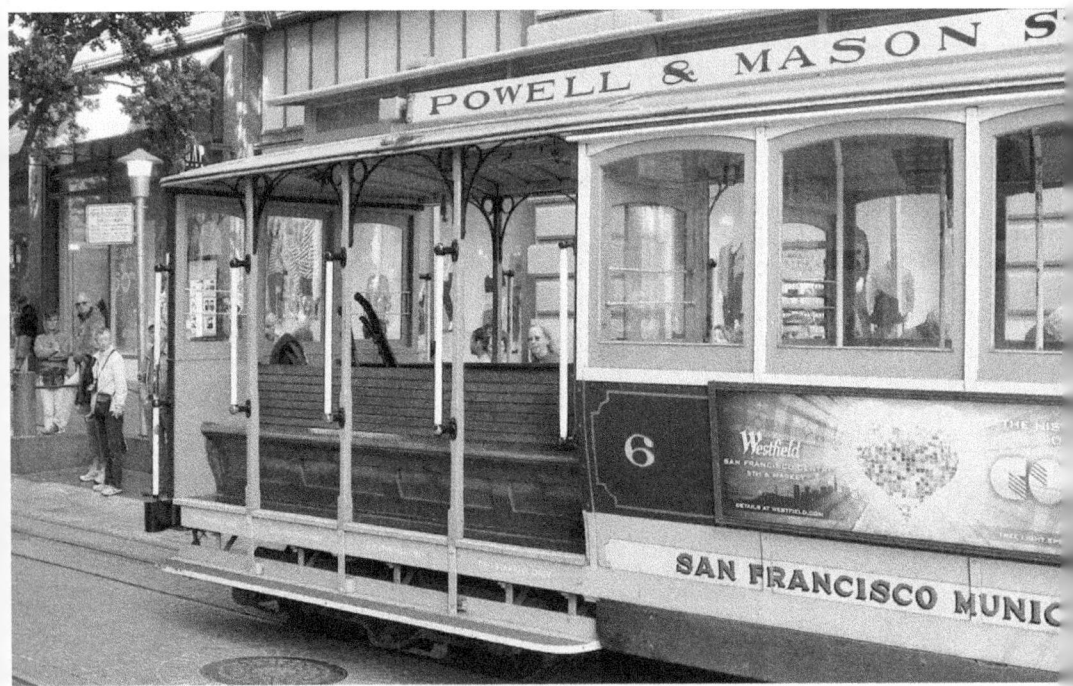

America,
       Cable cars on steep streets
       Glen Canyon, Twin Peaks
       Golden Gate, Bay Bridge
       Mount Tam in spring.

America,
       Edison, Morrison
       O'Keefe & Dr. King.

America,
       Shiner Bock, Enchanted Rock
       Alamo, Luckenbach
       Ruby's brisket BBQ
       Willie smokin' grass.

America,
       Stared down the Soviets
       & Kicked Nazi ass!

America,
       Amish country, Poconos
       Gettysburg battle woes
       Ben Franklin, Carnegie
       Mount Nittany.

America,
       Frightened by shadows
       & Syrian refugees.

America,
       Quaking in its boots,
       Sacrificing its soul
       For a mere illusion of
       Security.

If You Only Played Guitar

Maybe she never sang to you, or held you in her arms
Maybe your mom never nursed you, caused you lasting harm.
Maybe your father always yelled at you, starting in the womb
All I know is we all scram when you enter the room.
Yeah, your past might explain you, but only so far,
'Cause you wouldn't be such a smeghead if you only played guitar.

Think that you're so better than all of us
If we don't bow down, you make a big fuss.
All your petty little tantrums just wear us down
Can't you see us smirking, when you turn around?
No shipwright would ever describe you as yar,
But you wouldn't be such a smeghead if you only played guitar.

'Cause music's about life & death, love & loss
Rootin' for the little guy, against a callous boss.
You'd gain perspective, even grow your soul,
Begin to seek understanding of the world as a whole.
The lives of those around you perhaps less you'd scar
'Cause you wouldn't be such a smeghead if you only played guitar.

If you only played guitar, if you only played guitar
Wouldn't fix everything, but surely would go far.
Think that you're so grand? Well I hate to quibble:
No one can stand you – not even a tribble.
If you only played guitar, if you only played guitar
Wouldn't fix everything, but surely would go far.
Put down that report and pick up Lister's guitar!
You wouldn't be such a smeghead, Rimmer,
        if you only played guitar.

You couldn't remain so cold and unfeeling to your peers
If you'd played songs about others' dreams, hopes & fears.
Inhabited their heads, walked in their shoes
Caught a glimpse of how you give us the blues.
A long shot to think that you could come far
But surely less a smeghead if you only played guitar.

If you only played guitar, if you only played guitar
You wouldn't be such a smeghead if you only played guitar.
If you only played guitar, if you only played guitar
You wouldn't be such a smeghead –
Yeah, you wouldn't be such a smeghead! –
If you only played guitar.

I Couldn't Achieve World Peace

I couldn't achieve world peace
Or discover what it all means.
No passionate new lover
To fulfill all my dreams.
Fame & fortune too elusive
& Success left me behind,
But I've a new garbage disposal
& That's pretty damn fine.

Life Behind a Screen

Scurry through the art museum, snapping photos galore
See it all through my phone, then on to do more.
No chance to appreciate, can't even contemplate
Just record for posterity to them my proximity.

Chorus:
'Cause I'm living my life behind a screen
A digital filter to all that I've seen.
Experienced through a pixel display
Record it all for a future day.
Gotta share it online, just can't resist
Checking it got likes, so I know I exist.

Dare not look up from my phone I was using to record
My son's first hockey game, don't want to miss when he scored.
Can't pay attention to what's happening
Can't cheer or root, just have time to aim and shoot.

Chorus

Always dreamed of Yosemite, this year finally made it there.
Got to capture it all, every sight so rare.
Kids keep their voices low to not wreck the audio.
No time to soak it in, someday we'll appreciate it then.

Then one day while hiking, tripped over a rock
Phone smashed to pieces, boy was I in shock.
Had to see through my own eyes at the world all around
Colors were subtly different and the scale was all wrong.

I shook for a while, then slowly regained control,
Finally reached the top, a beautiful sunset to behold.
Couldn't share it or tweet it, nothing else to do,
But hold my wife & kids tight & enjoy it … just us few.

Echoes of Iowa

I grew up in northwest Iowa
Where sturdy farm folk
(Though I was a townie)
Would trudge through blizzards
And 20° below
To milk the cows
And feed the pigs
Out in the barn
Uphill both ways
And of course
No matter the weather
To church twice on Sundays.

I thought of them
As I finally schlepped
The bowls of compost
Collecting on the deck
Out to the bin
A full 30 yards away
– Braving mud and dog droppings –
Now that our inch of snow
Had fully melted
And feeling so
Robust
And hardy
In the process.

Tulip Time

Grab your quarters, grab your dollars
We're off to the Tulip Festival
Eat snowcones & *saucijzenbroodjes*
Never stop 'til we're all full.
Two free tickets for wearing Dutch clothes
An extra one for the wooden shoes.
We'll ride the Zoomer & the tilt-a-whirl
Then to the arcade, we've quarters to lose.

Chorus:
Wearing Dutch costumes, it's Tulip Time
Pigs in the Blanket, it's Tulip Time
Watching the parade, it's Tulip Time
We're going on the rides, it's Tulip Time!

You'll love the tulips full in bloom
This sleepy little town's sure come alive.
We've got a bank in the shape of a windmill
Snap a photo when you pass by.
Listen to the Amsterdam street organ,
While Dutch Dancers romp in their wooden shoes.
A loose meat sandwich from the Monica ladies
So many desserts, don't know how to choose.

Chorus

Grab a broom & a bucket of water
They're washing the streets, let's lend a hand.
Then sit on the curb and watch the parade
Brother plays tuba in the marching band.
See the Tulip Queen's float passing us by?
Sister's waving up there on the right.
Then eat cotton candy & go on more rides
We'll hang out here 'til they close for the night.

Chorus

The musical this year is *Fiddler on the Roof*
Dad plays Tevye like he's on Broadway.
See the flower show in the bank basement?
There's a blue ribbon on mom's bouquet!
A town like this doesn't have much to offer
We need this break from being austere.
By Monday morn it's all back to normal,
But we'll have even more fun come next year!

Chorus

Don't you just love it, it's Tulip Time!

23

City of Snow

Look out the window, it's the first big snow
By this time tomorrow, a whole city will grow.
The town needs a place to dump it all
So in our cornfield they pile it tall.
When the trucks finally go, we kids come
Build and explore until we're all numb.
With a big snow like this, there'll be some tall towers
We're freezing cold, yet stay out for hours.

It's our city of snow, our city of ice
It's new every time and sure does entice.
Snow plows dumped it all in the field
Now it's ours to discover what mystery's revealed.
You choose your castle & I'll choose mine
No adults out here to keep us in line.
It's all good out here …
It's all good out here, we're doing just fine!

Get out there first to claim the best pile
If it stays cold long, you'll have it a while.
Prepare for the inevitable epic battle
So build up your snowball arsenal.
Feeling ambitious? Bring your own shovel
Carve out a snow cave, dig out a tunnel.
On the tallest mound we play King of the Hill
Think that you're so tough? Come prove your skill.

Chase each other playing snowball tag
Late at night we try capture the flag.
One day we're on the trail of Soviet spies
Next fighting a World War, we're the Allies.
Let's do something exciting, do you dare?
There's buried treasure out there somewhere.
Be careful where you dig, you may find a surprise
It's said they dump the body here when someone dies.

It's our city of snow, our city of ice
It's new every time and sure does entice.
Snow plows dumped it all in the field
Now it's ours to discover what mystery's revealed.
You choose your castle & I'll choose mine
No adults out here to keep us in line.
It's all good out here …
It's all good out here, we're doing just fine!

A kid got lost out here, beware of his ghost
Or so we tell the new kids they listen engrossed.
But I nearly died here, one warm March day
A large lake formed, thought a new place to play.
Tried to cross it, but got my foot caught,
Couldn't release it no matter how hard I fought.
Stood there waist deep, feared I'd never get free
Caught a bad cold, was in bed for a week.

It's changed since my youth in so many ways
No longer get snows like that these days.
That field's long gone, now a Wal-Mart store,
And kids today spend their winters indoors.
Just stare at some brightly lit LED screen
On one of their many electronic machines.
Don't built forts or have snowball fights
Don't even sneak out and play at night.

It's our city of snow, our city of ice
It's new every time and sure does entice.
Snow plows dumped it all in the field
Now it's ours to discover what mystery's revealed.
You choose your castle & I'll choose mine
No adults out here to keep us in line.
It's all good out here …
It's all good out here, we're doing just fine!
It's all good out here … we're doing … just fine.

On Reading Sietze Buning

Huisbezoek
Dooyeweerdian
Heidelberg Catechism
Total Depravity
The Elect.
Phrases from my youth
Forgotten
Ignored
Return
Upon rereading
Sietze Buning's
Style and Class.

Orange City & Sioux Center
So conservative
So provincial
Yet at Northwestern College
(& perhaps at Dordt, too)
An academic
      Community
That I sometimes envy
Even at a major research university –
A quality that Sietze's dad
Might have called, simply,
Purpaleanie!

Note: Sietze Buning was the pen name for Calvin College
English professor Stanley Wiersma. His books
Purpaleanie and Other Permutations and *Style and Class*,
published by Middleburg Press, describe growing up on a farm
in Middleburg, Iowa, near Orange City & Sioux Center.

Computers - A Love Story

1975. As a little kid, try to make a 'computer' out of a cardboard box after seeing a computer on an episode of *Shazam!* (or was it *Isis?*). Disappointed that mine didn't do anything.

Fall 1980. First see a computer in person in seventh grade when a fellow Boy Scout brings in a chess-playing computer – just a circuit board, keyboard, and black & white monitor, but I am in love.

Spring 1981. Discover that my junior high in Princeton, NJ, has a computer class using Commodore PET microcomputers, which I beg to take. Instead, I get assigned to woodworking. (Dammit!)

Spring 1981. My mother, a Ph.D. student at Rutgers University, is using their mainframe computer for her research. She brings home punch cards that I treasure as sacred relics.

Fall 1981. Now in eighth grade & back in Iowa, I hang out at the local Radio Shack where a TRS-80 Color Computer is for sale. My efforts to get my parents to buy it are utterly unsuccessful.

Spring 1982. Gain access to the PDP-11 computer at Northwestern College and learn BASIC. Bring to school pages of dot-matrix printout (perforated, holed edges still attached) of this program:

```
10 PRINT "I HATE SCHOOL!"
20 GOTO 10
```

Earned me detention. Was worth it.

January 1983. Convince my parents to buy a Commodore 64 computer so I can do the statistics calculations my mother needs for her dissertation. For the two years, that machine was my life. I wrote super-fast machine language games & programs for it. I could tell you the function of specific memory locations. Other than its agonizingly slow floppy drive, it was pure heaven.

They sure don't make computers like that anymore.

Careless & Free

You'd drag me out of the house to explore
Tap on my window, I'd sneak out the backdoor
Wander through fields, take things apart
Race in your crude hacked-together go-cart
Through the secret back alleys of town
You knew everywhere, you sure got around.

How to kick the machine behind the garage just right
To snag a free can of Coke or Sprite.
Around you always some craziness swirled
You taught me about girls, expanded my world.
My parents warned me about being your friend
Why I hung out with you, they didn't comprehend.

But you were …
Pinned down by nothin', speech laced with cussin'
Had no obligation, your own creation.
You were the boy I wanted to be
Wild, crazy, careless & free.

In high school, you exuded such confidence
Thought you profound even when spouting nonsense.
You were quicker with words than anyone I knew
Recited Dylan Thomas and Faulkner, too.
Yet just a month before our graduation
You skipped town, made the road your vocation.

You'd crash my college, hadn't changed your ways,
Drag me out of the dorm, just like the old days.
The first few times, you made me less homesick
But by senior year, I came to resent it.
I had work to do, I had code to write
A career to prepare for, that goal in sight.

You were still …
Pinned down by nothin', speech laced with cussin'
Had no obligation, your own creation.
You were the boy I wanted to be
Wild, crazy, careless & free.

For the next five years, you went underground
You never called, never came around.
I was working long hours building my career,
Met a nice girl, a fellow engineer.
You were always fascinated by Townes
I hoped his road you hadn't gone down.

You had some electrifying stories to share
That day you finally surfaced, you'd answered my prayer.
All I could relate was my programming work
How I'd married Donna, how my boss was a jerk.
Donna never warmed to you despite your charm
Whenever you swept though, I sensed her alarm.

'Cause you were …
Pinned down by nothin', speech laced with cussin'
Had no obligation, your own creation.
You were the boy I wanted to be
Wild, crazy, careless & free.

I'm 34 now, with a wife and a son
When you showed up tonight at a quarter to one
Donna reminded me, and it was not a request
No longer were you a welcomed guest:
"He's a bad influence on your son just four.
You call this a life?" ask her eyes, and more.

'Cause she knows some days I feel like chucking it all
Quit my job and just jump over the wall.
She fears I'll join you out on the road
Ditch everything, all our lives implode.
As I look at you now on the sofa, snoring,
I realize this tension I can't keep ignoring.

Pinned down by nothin', speech laced with cussin'
Had no obligation, your own creation.
Are you the man I'd choose to be?
Wild, crazy, careless & free?

I wonder: Are you truly living or am I?
Do I envy or pity you, and if so why?
Is your frenetic pace how you embrace life,
Or just your way to avoid real strife?
Are you always running so no one can get
Close enough to hurt you, so you never commit?

Am I afraid that you will rub off on my son,
Or that you won't 'cause you'll be long gone?
Our divergent paths now permanently split
I'm settled in a world in which you don't fit.
You're a part of me, man, but I'm afraid you gotta go
When you wake up, you've got to hit the road.
When you wake up, time to hit the road.

Pinned down by nothin', speech laced with cussin'
Have no obligation, your own creation.
You were the boy I wanted to be
Wild, crazy, careless & free.

Random Artifacts from High School

Me (indignantly) in history class: "Why weren't people concerned about pollution when they started driving cars?"
Mr. Regnerus: "Oh, they were very concerned about pollution – specifically, what all the horses were dropping on the roads!"
This is the only thing I recall from four years of high school history and it's a gem – it taught me a lot about perspective.

My religion teacher saw occult forces at work in the world and once warned me about meditation: "Each word has a demon attached to it, so if you meditate, you'll conjure up the demon associated with your mantra and it will possess your soul." I wondered: If you invent a new word, is a new demon created, too? (If so, Shakespeare has much to atone for!) Or are there bored demons sitting on a bench somewhere in hell waiting for new words to be invented? Is there a separate demon for cat, *gato*, *chat*, *Katze*? What about homonyms like one & won?

Mr. S____ claimed we wouldn't dare walk through the graveyard at midnight on Halloween, so of course we had to do it. When a police car entered the cemetery at the far end and drove slowly in our direction, we sprinted back to our car parked on the street. My shoes were untied (a fad at the time) and halfway to the car one of my shoes fell off, so I had to go back for it. I dived into the car & shut the door an instant before the police car crested a hill inside the cemetery by the exit and its headlights shone directly into our rear window. They lingered for a worryingly long time as we crouched low in the car. I started tying my shoes after that.

The school's "computer room" had two Apple IIe computers and we would take turns playing Castle Wolfenstein, Microsoft's Olympic Decathlon, and writing BASIC programs on them. Mr. K____, the physical science teacher, came in one day with a floppy disk asking for my help. He had earlier made a chemistry crossword puzzle for his class, but couldn't remember the password to open the file again. "I just know that it's not H [for Hydrogen]. Could be He." The crossword program document was a simple ASCII text file with the password as its first line – which, of course, was H.

Facing Walls

Homecoming.
One wall of the hallway:
Glittering Bibles, crosses, doves
& "God is love."
Facing side:
"Kill, kill, kill!"
To Mr. G_____, the Principal
(I had dragged him from his office)
"Explain," I demanded,
He sighed & just shrugged.

In God, no slave nor free,
Yet each fall, school-sanctioned Slave Day:
Freshmen enslaved to Seniors
(most boys forced to wear dresses, culminating in
a slave show with a judging panel of seniors) –
Public humiliation for the day.

"Without it, bullying would be worse," Mr. V_____ says,
Ignoring the fact that bullies always push beyond
Authority-set boundaries, no matter how broad.
"Besides, it's all just for fun."

Recently thinking back to high school
For the first time in probably 25 years,
Suddenly remember this ritual & wonder,
"This didn't really happen, did it?"
"How was this ever allowed?!"
"What the fuck were the grown-ups thinking?!"
But friends from back then I asked confirmed it
And remembered it far better than had I,
Even sent me old yearbook photos,
        Documentary proof,
To show me what I couldn't believe I had forgotten:
One year the slave-judging senior panel
        All decked out in
                White hoods.

The Pulpit

Be careful that you speak the truth
For you face Christ Himself –
His left hand reached out to bless
'Gainst sword-pierced side right pressed.

Robed wholly in glory's shine
Yet mere cloth around his waist
As for your soul – and mine – He died
A gift given of God's grace.

Above you, His angelic mother
Mary stands undeterred
Below you esteemed preachers
Pondering God's Holy Word.
Disciples sleep & Jesus prays
The night before His Passion
Women weep 'til the third day
& St. George slays the dragon.

You stand on a narrow pedestal
Sustained by Saints from long ago
Too small it seems by human means
But on the weak God strength bestows.

The earthly & the sinful
Aim to lead His flock astray
So God placed a guard dog here
To keep salamanders & toads at bay.
Alone those inspired by Trinity
May rise in wheels of three,
And the elements four
Of this imperfect sphere
Roll down these stairs austere.

My creation, but you'll never know
Who I was back then
For I built it for God's glory
Not vain adoration of men.
But I snuck a little piece of me
In sandstone, my face,
So I could keep an eye on things
From down here near the base.

House of Sinners & Saints

Jake plays an ace, the fifth in the deck
Nicotine patches, he looks like a wreck.
Dirk draws a gun & pulls the trigger
But was his hand, his index finger.
Says, "Was a time when your tricks couldn't miss."
Then 'bout some old conquest they reminisce.

Joe's brothers beat him & left him for dead
'Cause he was dad's favorite, given fancy new threads.
Years later they've found him, now their lives in his hands
Joe's made it big here and famine's ravaged their lands.
He wants to make 'em suffer, send them off to die,
But instead he embraces them, and together they all cry.

Come in one, come in all,
God knows at times we all fall.
Accepted here for who we are
Grace reaches us, no matter how far
We run or how dark our soul's taints
Here in the House of Sinners & Saints.

Late one night Tony sits by a prostitute
Offers her a drink she looks so destitute.
"Just turned my birthday, and nobody gives a damn,"
She cries, "Only the same old being pawed & slammed."
Tony buys balloons & bakes a birthday cake
Goes back to that bar to help her celebrate.

Turns out Sonya's run away from home,
Now here she knows she's not alone.
Heavy metal Janie, all spikes and tattoos
Knits her a sweater with Sally goody-two-shoes.
Joe & Johnny play a Redemption Song
None of them question whether they belong.

Come in one, come in all,
God knows at times we all fall.
Accepted here for who we are
Grace reaches us, no matter how far
We run or how dark our soul's taints
Here in the House of Sinners & Saints.

The King preaches justice & not only in the pews
While Nicholas sneaks money to the poor in their shoes.
"Think we need everything right now," laments Jacques.
"It's all propaganda," he says. "We need punk rock!"
Gus prays for chastity but not yet –
Starting tomorrow; tonight, he wants Babette.

"Go sin boldly," preaches our brother Luther.
"But trust even more boldly, it's not cheap grace on offer."
'Cause "When Christ calls a man, he calls him to die,"
Writes Herr Bonhoeffer and to the end he complies.
Yes, on our life together, Dietrich would reflect
But he gave up his own, for others' lives to protect.

Come in one, come in all,
God knows at times we all fall.
Accepted here for who we are
Grace reaches us, no matter how far
We run or how dark our soul's taints
Here in the House of Sinners & Saints.

With us not the mighty Francis comes to sup
Sits with the downtrodden man who's shown up.
Myriel gives his silver to save a soul
Makes both him and that thief whole.
Yes, in God's love we've all come to trust
So we pick up each other & shake off the dust.

Here in the House of Sinners & Saints
Here in the House of Sinners & Saints.

Just Call Me Job

My lucky Lotto number just hit the jackpot
Of course, this once, I hadn't bought
Given all my cash to a friend in need
Never goes unpunished, does a good deed.

Chorus:
The world's out to get me, the universe's against me,
Sometimes I think I'm just gonna explode.
In some past life, whom did I piss?
Must have sinned greatly to be treated like this.
Just call me Job.

Slowpoke ahead, I sure wish he were dead
Limit's 45, going 25 instead.
"Wake up & drive!" each minute I've pled
And every frickin' light is red.

Waiting to check out, woman cuts in front
I had a small basket, she had a cart full.
After five price checks she pulls out a wad
At least 50 coupons, and I cry out to God.

Chorus

Stuck here in this airport, now missed my damn flight
Rest are all full, probably stuck here tonight.
Hotels all booked, not a bed free for miles
Useless airline staff – so sick of fake smiles.

Reading the news feed, as I curse out my plane
A derailed freight train, a war in Ukraine
A bird flu scare, a tsunami somewhere …
Oh, why am I stuck here? It just ain't no fair!

Chorus

Just call me Job.

Motorcycle Man of God

He's a motorcycle man of God
On a massive Harley you'll find Rod
Across the country he does ride
The Word of God by his side.

He sat beside me at the bar
At the time I had fallen far
On the edge of a precipice
Gonna end it after getting pissed.
He ordered a beer & turned to me
Said, "That's a dangerous place to be."

"Once sitting on that very stool,
I was gonna leave this world cruel
And I see that same thought in you
So the dark I came to see you through.
I ain't here to judge, condemn,
'Cause I know God loves you, my friend."

He's a motorcycle man of God
On a massive Harley you'll find Rod
Across the country he does ride
The Word of God by his side.

"You don't know my story, pal,
All I did that lost me my gal.
Then my family & job –
Out there probably a lynch mob.
No one can love me, mate,
So just leave me to drink my fate."

"Afraid I can't do that, Brother,
For I'm sent from your Holy Mother
& The past is just that, the past
Now lean on God's love so vast.
Come my friend, together we'll pray
For strength for another day."

He's a motorcycle man of God
On a massive Harley you'll find Rod
Across the country he does ride
The Word of God by his side.

As the hour approached dawn
& All other patrons had gone,
He gave the bartender a nod,
Who replied, "Catch you later, Rod."
As I heard him ride away fast,
Wondered what led him down this path?
His tattoos might have told the tale
Where he found God, probably jail.

As I got up to face the day
I heard the bartender say:
"Would you believe he was once named Jane?
But rejected when she began to change.
One night sat where you had been
Drowning herself for what they called sin.
Then the voice of God spoke in her head:
'I love you for you,' it said."

" 'Rod, I see you as you truly are
& For me you're gonna travel far.'
Now he searches for troubled souls
Helping them to become whole.
Like Jesus on the cross,
A shepherd finding we sheep lost."

He's a motorcycle man of God
Was Jane, but now he's called Rod.
Across the country he does ride
The word of God by his side.
A motorcycle man of Christ
Might have just saved my life
Not sure where to go from here,
But for once not consumed by fear.
Yeah, he's a motorcycle man of God
On a massive Harley you'll find Rod.

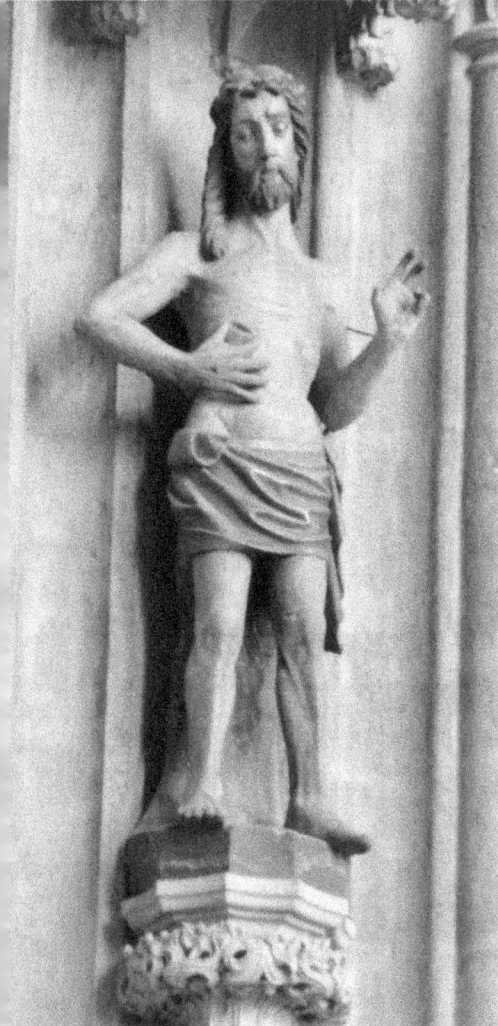

Fellow Christian

No atheist has ever convinced me
To abandon faith in God.
No adherent of another faith
Has tempted me from mine.
But what drives me away
Is you, fellow Christian,
And the hate that you display.

As a kid we sang together:
  "They will know
   We are Christians
   By our love,"
But it seems a quality
That neither of us shows
Nearly enough.

Summary of the Law

Eloquently you stated
Two concise laws:
Love Me with your whole heart
& Your neighbor as yourself.

Such beautiful sentiments,
Too bad they'll never work
'Cause you seem rather needy
& My neighbor's a real jerk.

God's Editor

Thanks for coming in, God.
Your Bible – why it's brilliant.
They'll be talking about it for millennia!
It'll be a best seller, I guarantee it.
But I have a few concerns. In brief:
        It's scattered in its format,
        Inconsistent in its style &
        Muddled in its message.

Your innovative idea
of having a different co-author for nearly every chapter
has given the Bible an eclectic feel,
but it's also made it difficult
to get a good sense
of what you wish to convey.
Did they all get the same memo?
The same talking points?
I think a few might have gone rogue.

And, frankly, you've buried the lead so much that
one can't tell what you think is most important!
Early on, you give all these rules for eating –
Eat this, but not that, like you had in mind a diet book –
And then later you say, "Ha, just kidding!
I didn't really care about that after all."
Are you just messing with us?!

And what's with these long, painfully detailed descriptions
of the Ark of the Covenant and sacrificial rules?
I mean, seriously?
Snooze time!
You've lost your reader until at least
the walls of Jericho come down –
if they haven't given up long before then.
Perhaps Victor Hugo as ghostwriter
wasn't the best choice here –
It felt like his dissertation on the sewers of Paris.

Speaking of the Jericho story:
Neat gimmick with the trumpets –
No one will believe it, of course,
but it's fiction after all, so that's okay.
But slaughtering everyone in the city?
Did you really mean that?
I'm just saying because later you've got your Jesus fellow
talking about loving enemies and turning cheeks.
You're going to utterly confuse your reader.

Maybe your protagonist,
this Jesus,
can summarize it all somewhere.
Like in *Bill & Ted's Excellent Adventure*:
   "Be Excellent to Each Other &
   Party On, Dude!"
Nothing complicated.
Be sure to rewrite them a bit, of course,
so you don't get sued.
Still, Jesus comes in the story so late that
I worry by then the reader won't pick up on His importance
or pay close attention to what He says.
Their heads will still be back in Leviticus
worrying about what's an abomination and what's not.

I'm just asking you to be clear about what you are saying:
Like animal sacrifices – do you want them or not?
Getting a tattoo – sinful or not?
Mixing types of cloth or seeds in a field? Eating shellfish?
I'm not here to tell you *what* to say, Heaven forbid,
just to help you say it *better.*
After all, if people don't understand what you want to convey,
then we've all failed, right?

Just a few more items I've noted:
In Genesis, can you pick just one Creation story?
And add a note that it's a figurative, not historical, treatment?
Yeah, I guess you're right –
No one could believe that you meant it literally.

About Ecclesiastes –
"Vanity of vanity, all is vanity" –
Really depressing stuff.
Did you have to hire Dostoevsky for that?

Now Job has promise.
I like this Satan character
(You should use him more!),
but the conversations do drag on.
Okay, I get that Job got a raw deal,
but does he have to whinge on about it so?
And, frankly, your answer to him
is hardly going to satisfy your reader.

Now getting Danielle Steele to work with you on
Song of Solomon was inspired –
Really hot steamy stuff there!
Can we do more like this?
Maybe give Jezebel a larger role?

Oh, and we've got to talk about this Paul dude.
Some great writing there, really powerful stuff –
They'll be quoting Romans 8 for centuries –
but what's his beef with women?
It's too bad that he's so bitter about not getting dates,
but he's going to turn off women readers
and they're our biggest market these days.

About the prophets – There are just too many of them
and they keep saying the same things over and over again.
They complain that the people don't listen to them,
but maybe it's because they are too long-winded.
Let's cut the minor prophets
and reduce each of the rest to his elevator pitch, something like,
"Stop worshipping other gods
& don't be such jerks to each other"?

Speaking of not worshipping other gods:
How is this Ba'al guy related to Satan – are they brothers?
Father & son? Comrades? Competitors?

And what about Ashtoreh? Where does she fit in to the mix?
Are they lesser gods? Fallen angels? What's their feud with God?
Will this backstory appear in a prequel someday?

Also, did you realize that your co-author for the final chapter,
Revelations, was tripping on LSD as he wrote?
I fear nut jobs will mine it for all kinds of apocalyptic shit
& incite some perilous "end of the world" hysteria.
(Let's not repeat Orson Welles' *War of the Worlds*, shall we?)

Overall, God you've got some great stories here –
I love Noah's Ark with the animals and the rainbow
      (kids will eat it up – despite the genocide by flood),
Jonah and the whale (inspired by Pinocchio?),
Adam & Eve & the snake (a hint of Gabriel García Márquez there),
the epic tale of King David (very Arthurian!),
the whole Moses-Pharaoh-plague-Passover story
      (a riveting sibling rivalry with a dramatic aquatic ending!),
and Daniel in that lion's den (good excitement for the kiddies).
Gripping stuff!
If you keep all this and ditch much of the rest,
you'll have a real page turner on your hands.

Before you leave to write the 2nd draft,
let's just recall the KISS rule a moment –
Keep it Short and Simple. People like quick reads.
Short books are good in the bathroom and perfect for the beach.
People may buy long books but they don't read them –
they just put them on the shelf for show.
As it is now, no one will slog through the whole thing –
They'll just selectively pick out bits and pieces
that fit what they want to hear (context be damned).

I know as the Creator, you feel you've got a lot to say.
But they'll remember more if you say less.
Word to the wise?

Lady Jane

Lady Jane Below Stairs the Muse's gift & curse,
For Lovejoy knew not from where came chorus & verse.
His biggest hit by far, each word fans did know
Yelling, demanding, he play it every show.

But no more could he sing it, its chords he would not strum
Void where its spark once lit, now just left him numb.
One evening on the road, a rare night with no show
He took a walk – but to find what? Even he did not know.

"For Lady Jane found both her dreams and nightmares
Salvation & damnation, that night below stairs."

He wandered into Webster's, a basement coffee shop,
An open mike in progress, to listen he did stop.
No one recognized him, though Jim the host did ask,
"Are you going to play tonight?" "I think I'll pass."

Later a girl with teal hair, scrawny, about 18,
Approached him, "I'm Elaine, I'm up next to sing."
"I need someone on guitar," she said, but why choose him?
"I have no guitar," he said. "Borrow mine," said Jim.

Against his better judgment, he got up on the stage,
A song that once had saved her she said they would play.
Had spoken to her despair when she thought all in vain –
A kindred spirit to help her bear the pain was Lady Jane.

"For Lady Jane found both her dreams and nightmares
Salvation & damnation, that night below stairs."

She'd tricked him & he knew it, but couldn't help but play along,
For when she starting singing, knew to her his song belonged.
His fingers flowed like satin, each string felt of silk,
Her voice rang down to Hades, sustained like Heaven's milk.

The song was passing through him, no longer from his head,
The Muse had come to recall him to the place where she'd once led.
& Before him she stood there, a vision, Lady Jane,
On that eve when so much she would lose & gain.

"For Lady Jane found both her dreams and nightmares
Salvation & damnation, that night below stairs."

"In fear & hope she trembled, her lips shared sin and prayer
He felt her chest pounding that night below stairs.
The rush of forbidden passion, the breath on her neck wet
Knowing this first time their last, each taste desperate."

"To escape her velvet prison for the mystery beyond that door,
The promise of adventure, a cry for something more."
Every soul enraptured, a spell together weaved,
All living in that moment, its truth felt, believed.

"For Lady Jane found both her dreams and nightmares
Salvation & damnation, that night below stairs."

He handed the guitar back to Jim, on her forehead kissed Elaine
Without a word walked out of there, still humming Lady Jane.

"For Lady Jane found both her dreams and nightmares
Salvation & damnation, that night below stairs."

DOWN the Shore
everything's alright

NO
SWIMMING

Three Drams, Four

Our pubs gone dry, our throats are parched,
Our liquid soul's been shipped away
For food and arms to fight the war,
Not a dram of whiskey to be found.
Every bottle to America bound in that
Ship sailing past our island shore.
Then Polly hit the reef one day
In the Sound of Eriskay.

Now it's 1 dram, 2 drams, 3 drams, 4
We've sure got whiskey galore.
For once we couldn't want for more,
Except our boys come home from war.
God bless that beautiful Polly.

The S.S. Politician,
Polly to her friends,
Warmed our hearts this February 1941.
Single malts second to none
For a while we'll be merry
'Til the whiskey ends, pray
The war's over by then.

Now it's 1 dram, 2 drams, 3 drams, 4
We've sure got whiskey galore.
For once we couldn't want for more,
Except our boys come home from war.
God bless that beautiful Polly.

They'd expelled many like us to Canada,
Leveled shacks and let sheep run.
Factor said we're in the way
Of some distant far-off lord
Who never came here, our needs ignored.
Barely scraped by, but we still stayed.
A small repayment for all they'd done
To us still left on these islands.

Oh yeah, it's 1 dram, 2 drams, 3 drams, 4
We've sure got whiskey galore.
For once we couldn't want for more,
Except our boys come home from war.
God bless that beautiful Polly.

We risked our lives on that icy sea
Now our bounty they try to seize.
We just took what had been left to
Drown for good, can't call that theft.
The excise men now come around
To confiscate all whiskey found,
But by our hands was liberated
So our own throats get lubricated.

With 1 dram, 2 drams, 3 drams, 4
We've sure got whiskey galore.
For once we couldn't want for more,
Except our boys come home from war.
God bless that beautiful Polly.

Sisi

If only in Bad Ischl, he'd not fallen for me
Sister Néné would have relished this role that I can't be.
15,000 candles lit, a flame that did destroy
Sobbing at my wedding, 'twere not tears of joy.
Just a carefree teenage girl when crowned me *Kaiserin*
& Told me I exist to give a male heir to him.

Once again Franz Joseph asks, "What can I make of you?
Oh Sisi, oh Sisi?" he says but has no clue.

Into these chains of vanity wish I'd never strayed[1]
Titania must not remain jailed in this gilded cage.
For I do so long in vain for the kingdom of my dreams[2]
To be a seagull flying over waves of sunlit gleams.[3]
For the open sea is freedom, in one place I cannot dwell
If I had to stay anywhere even paradise my hell.[4]

Again & again they ask, "What can we make of you?
Oh Sisi, oh Sisi?" they say but have no clue.

The Hofburg & the Schönbrunn wish I'd play the Empress more,
But all their Habsburg intrigues, for me *ein todlich* bore.
I know my ladies-in-waiting are there to spy on me
Ha! But I'm the one who reveals in my poetry.
I couldn't find meaning in my motherhood
For my Sophie died so young, killed himself my only son.

Once again Franz Joseph asks, "What can I make of you?
Oh Sisi, oh Sisi?" he says but has no clue.

"Ich bin ein Kind der Sonne,[5]" the only God that I can see
Place my faith here on Earth in freedom & beauty.
At Prime, three hours of worship to the perfection of my hair,
My gymnasium my chapel, exercise my daily prayer.
I'll climb the Schmittenhöhe, love cold as the Pasterze,
Feel my legs 'gainst the saddle horn, only then can I breathe free.

And once beauty has faded and freedom eluded me
Then will call my final rest at the bottom of the deepest sea.

Again & again they ask, "What can we make of you?
Oh Sisi, oh Sisi?" they say but have no clue.

The world I see but from afar,
   "Alone, I stand, as on a star.[6]"
One that once shone in my hair,
   now only black I wear.
A needle file in Geneva,
   wielded for anarchy
I fell into my dear Irma's arms,
   Titania could finally flee[7]
Back to those Bavarian hills once
   Cousin Ludwig reigned;
Perhaps the same madness had
   Run through both our veins.
On my death adored me so,
   my life they did excuse,
For now could finally stuff me
   in the cage I had refused.

But *König & Kaiser* a silly game,
   a truth they could not see
'Til a Sarajevo bullet killed
   the whole damn monarchy.

Note: Empress Elisabeth (Sisi) was a poet and "Sisi" draws
upon imagery, quotes, and paraphrases from her writings:
[1]Poem dated May 8, 1854, two weeks after her wedding
[2]*"To My Master,"* 1887
[3]*Nordsee Lieder,* 1887
[4]Letter to Constantin Christomanos, quoted in Katrin Unterreiner's
 Sisi - Mythos und Wahrheit (2005).
[5]*"Ich bin ein Sonntagskind," Winterlieder,* 1887
[6]*To Future Souls,* 1887
[7]Poem on display in the Sisi Museum in the Hofburg, Vienna, Austria

Franz Joseph

What to make of Franz Joseph?
Honest, Loyal
Dullard, Dedicated?
So absorbed in minutia as to
Miss the historic movements
That would sweep his world away?
Cuckolded by none yet by all
Sophia's puppet
Then Sisi's lapdog
Finally, Bismark & Wilhelm's whipping boy.

Der Ewige – The Eternal – Kaiser, they say
As he oversaw the collapse
Of the unsaveable
The medieval Habsburg
Falling to the modern,
The noble to the nationalist
The human to the machine
The stuffy to the crass.

His son Rudolf saw the future &
Put himself out of his misery.
His wife Sisi saw it, too &
In neutral Switzerland
Made her own exit plans.
(Franz Joseph, had you
Imagination enough to see it coming, too?)

From absolute in 1848
To *K&K* of a diminished land
Military misadventures &
Political scheming far out of his league.
A bulwark against the Prussian project –
One that would lead down the darkest of roads –
Yet declared the war that would
Shatter Austria & Europe, and
Leave millions upon millions cold.

What to make of you, Franz Joseph?
In Vienna, where your statues abound
Remnants of a past glory
Like the Hofburg & your Opera House.
An autocrat from the age of kings,
Though you meant well, I do not doubt,
But how to resolve that, *Geliebter Kaiser*,
With how things
Eventually
Turned out?

Double V

For its million readers 'cross the country,
The *Pittsburgh Courier* spoke for liberty.
Covered what other papers did ignore
Like John Robinson, the Brown Condor.
And heroic deeds of black soldiers:
Like Dorie Miller at Pearl Harbor.
Robert Vann, its Editor,
Agitated for a black air corp.
(From Tuskegee, they went to war.)

The *Courier* started a movement in WW II
When James C. Thompson wrote in '42:
"Shall I sacrifice my life to then
Only live half American?
Yes, I demand after I fight for you
To have the same rights that you do.
So take this letter to be my decree,
It's time to fight for a double V."
(Yeah, fight for a double Victory!)

He said, "We're fighting for the Double V, won't settle for a single Victory.
Fight 'gainst fascism across this Earth and right here in the land of my birth.
Won't quit 'til we all are free, 'til Jim Crow's fled our Democracy."

We betray our liberty as a fraud
If we allow at home what we fight abroad.
Both Hitler and Jim Crow we'll confront
As we fight for democracy on two fronts,
'Gainst Hirohito and Mussolini,
Hear others' cries to be free.
Breathe life in Jefferson's Declaration
Of all created equal in our nation.
(Democracy at home & abroad.)

They said, "We're fighting for the Double V, won't settle for a single Victory.
Fight 'gainst fascism across this Earth and right here in the land of my birth.
Won't quit 'til we all are free, 'til Jim Crow's fled our Democracy."

Across America spread the Double V
Eleanor Roosevelt an enlistee.
Photos of people making the VV sign
Both black and white, no color line.
Had Double V posters, Double V pins,
Those V's stuck together just like twins.
Double V dances, Double V games,
Double V speakers who'd proclaim:
"Democracy at home & abroad!"

We're fighting for the Double V, won't settle for a single Victory.
Fight 'gainst fascism across this Earth and right here in the land of my birth.
Won't quit 'til we all are free, 'til Jim Crow's fled our Democracy.

The *Courier* pushed for integration
& Highlighted frequent discrimination.
Army said would be bad for morale
(Except if you were black & not treated well).
Banned it from libraries on Army bases
Said, "For freedom," with straight faces.
Tried to indict Editors for sedition,
Claimed the Double V was treason.
(Speaking truth the real reason.)

We're fighting for the Double V, won't settle for a single Victory.
Fight 'gainst fascism across this Earth and right here in the land of my birth.
Won't quit 'til we all are free, 'til Jim Crow's fled our Democracy.

Won't settle for a single Victory
We're fighting for the Double V!

Past & Future Me

I was watching a documentary
From long before my time
Back in the '50s and '60s
During the fight for civil rights.
Why, if I'd been alive then,
A Freedom Rider I'd have been
Beaten by cops in Selma,
Marched on Washington.

Then I noticed standing behind
The screaming mob of white
Was another crowd even larger,
Watching, taking in the sight,
& In that crowd awaited
A shock for me that night
For the spitting image of me
There I did find, &
Then that Past Me and Present Me
Connected across time.

And I sensed that Past Me
Was a respectable, good man:
Loving husband to his wife
Doting father to his kids
Worked hard at his job
In his church tithed 10%.
Never donned a white robe
No hatred in his bones
Never used the N-word
Yelled or threw stones.
But in the winds of change
His sails he had furled,
Didn't need agitators
Rocking his ordered world.

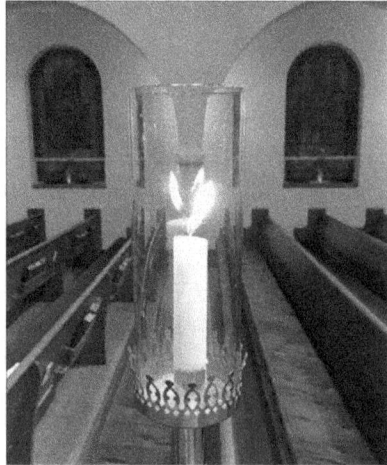

So I called to him:
"Past Me, oh Past Me,
Oh what did you do?
Didn't you fight for freedom,
For justice, too?
Why were you so deaf
To oppression's outcry?
To others' suffering, why did
You turn a blind eye?
Allowed your comfort to numb you
& Be seduced into the view
That there was simply nothing,
Nothing you could – or should – do?"

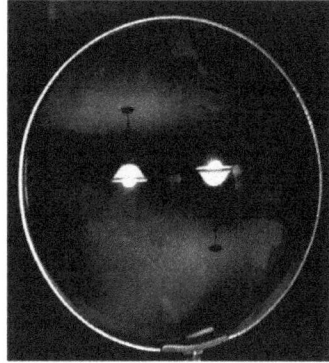

Then Past Me replied,
"You just don't understand.
You don't know how it is. I'm just one man.
It's the system & I can't change it,
These problems I cannot solve.
Busy enough with work & family,
I can't afford to get involved."

A challenge to his excuses
I was about to send his way
When I heard a new voice come to me,
Heard some Future Me say:
"Past Me, oh Past Me,
Oh what did you do?
Didn't you fight for freedom,
For justice, too?
Why were you so deaf
To oppression's outcry?
To others' suffering, why did
You turn a blind eye?
Allowed your comfort to numb you
& Be seduced into the view
That there was simply nothing,
Nothing you could – or should – do?"

I couldn't help but wonder,
How am I like me back then?
Whose oppression am I ignoring?
Is my silence a grave sin?
So I opened my eyes
To truly look around
And the suffering I witnessed
Did deeply astound.
But I saw more than I wanted,
And far more than I dared
So I closed my eyes again
Before in it I was snared.

Then to Future Me I replied,
"You just don't understand.
You don't know how it is. I'm just one man.
It's the system & I can't change it,
These problems I cannot solve.
Busy enough with work & family,
I can't afford to get involved."

Then in unison,
Past & Present Me
To our Future Self we called:
"We are good men,
The Lord knows it,
But can't afford
To get involved."

Bonhoeffer

For my son Dietre

I named you after Dietrich Bonhoeffer
In the hope that the evil he faced
Was forever in the past &
Would never rise again.

When we visited Flossenbürg KZ
Just two years ago
Where Bonhoeffer was murdered
On Hitler's personal order
I never thought that we'd see
This evil begin spreading
        over our own land
(As though the costly lessons
        from 70 years ago
Had been forgotten, unlearned).

I named you after Dietrich Bonhoeffer
In the uncertain (but sincere)
        conviction
That if I had lived then
I would have made
        the tough moral choice
That he and von Dohnányi faced
(Yet suspecting that I would have
Made the easy, comfortable
        one instead).

And, most of all
In the hope that I'd never
Have to find out.

Refugee

Buckled in tight, visa clutched in one hand
Headed towards freedom in a new land.
Translator for our troops in Iraq
& We swore we'd have his back
But at home their lives in grave peril
Collaborator with the American devil.
Had to wait so long, but finally came this day,
His little boy beside him, smiling away.

Behind them a widow, whose husband had died
Fighting al-Qaeda when a bomb on the roadside
Blew him to pieces, through her heart a knife,
Now flying to America to forge a new life.
But they came down the aisle in uniforms grey
And kicked them all right off of that plane:
"Trump's signed the order, your kind's no longer
Welcome in the U. S. of A."

We've dismantled Lady Liberty, built a wall in her place.
Sign says, "Go home, we've shut the gates!"
No comfort for the oppressed, no hospitality,
No shelter in America for the refugee.

Fleeing civil war, a young Syrian girl,
Badly burned by an exploding shell
Family all killed in a Russian-bombed hell
Church sponsored her to help her get well.
One flight towards freedom, one flight away from fear,
But the news came & brought her to tears:
"Trump's signed an order & so you've been banned
From America's shores, the promised land."

They've dismantled Lady Liberty, built a wall in her place.
Sign says, "Go home, we've shut the gates!"
No comfort for the oppressed, no hospitality,
No shelter in America for the refugee.

But that little girl was more than she seemed
Was Jesus returned in our fragile form
To check up on those His blood had redeemed
We whom He had so long ago warned:
"I was hungry, and you gave me no meat
I was thirsty and you gave me no drink
I was a stranger and you didn't take me in."
My soul quakes in fear at what Jesus did think.

For we've dismantled Lady Liberty, built a wall in her place.
Sign says, "Go home, we've shut the gates!"
No comfort for the oppressed, no hospitality,
No shelter in America for the refugee.
No comfort for the oppressed, no hospitality,
No shelter in America for the refugee.

Mark of Cain

His eighteenth birthday when cops stopped him
Just having some fun with his best friend.
Cops planted drugs, beat him up,
Booked for possession, locked him up.
"You're in big trouble, your situation's grim,
Got two choices," they told him.
"Take felony probation & we'll let you go free,
Else spend ten years in a penitentiary."

Now he's got a record, a permanent stain,
Forever yoked with his mark of Cain.
Tried to get a job 'til he could no longer bear
How they'd see that box checked and give him a hard stare.
Said "I'll work hard," but it was always the same:
No further questions, no chance to explain.
No one sees him behind that scarlet F,
His future been stolen, he's been left bereft.

Turn your head, avert your eyes,
He's an invisible man, ignore if you're wise.
Couldn't hear his story if it he did say,
But he's given up trying to share anyway.
Go write him off, he's only a felon,
Just forget that he's some mother's son.

Rain pours down hard, often in sheets,
Banned from public housing so lives on the streets.
No help for a felon, not even food stamps,
Some days so hungry, his stomach sure cramps.
Dreamed of school, but now the chances are slim,
There's no aid for a felon like him.
Stripped his rights, even stolen his vote,
Rain so hard, barely able to float.

Turn your head, avert your eyes,
He's an invisible man, ignore if you're wise.
Couldn't hear his story if it he did say,
But he's given up trying to share anyway.
Go write him off, he's only a felon,
Just forget that he's some mother's son.

No one will hire him, only the thugs,
In desperation, takes to selling drugs.
Costs him 10 solid years in the pen
Now 30 years old & life's a dead end.
Doesn't want your pity, just the life they did take,
Mark washed clean, from this nightmare awake.
At first glance, a hardened man on the skids;
Look more closely & you'll find that scared kid.
Deep inside he's still that scared kid …

Who's been set up, been beat up,
His future's been blown up,
He's grown up, now fed up,
Over having been f'd up.

Write him off, it's too late for him,
Nothing you can do, his future's dim.
Just thank the Lord that it's him not you,
The roll of the dice could have made it you, too.
What's his name, I don't even know,
'Cause there's thousands like him, I'm afraid so.
Forever burdened with their Mark of Cain,
Won't wash off, no matter how hard the rain.
Won't wash off, no matter how hard the rain.
Won't wash off, no matter how hard the rain.

Denora, PA

In Denora, near Pittsburgh, the U.S. Steel Zinc Works
Day & night sulfur-filled smoke spewing out,
Killing all the fish in the Monongahela River
& Eating the paint right off of our house.

In late October, 1948,
In a stagnant air layer, those fumes concentrate.
Soon we could chew on that bronze gritty smog,
My Pa coughing hard in that foul toxic fog.

Denora, Denora, we weep for our dead.
"Clean air or a paycheck," is all that they said.

The hospital was overrun, Pa could not breathe,
Firemen carted O_2, we were told to flee.
But couldn't leave town 'cause couldn't see to drive
Soon father & nineteen others had died.

Denora, Denora, we weep for our dead.
"Clean air or a paycheck," is all that they said.

Still the mills kept belching their smog born of greed
As we were dying they ignored our pleas.
Stopped only hours before cleansing rains came
Though was their exhaust they denied all blame.

Denora, Denora, we weep for our dead.
"Clean air or a paycheck," is all that they said.

But showed the world that air pollution could kill
Some even called it "Murder by Mill."
Denora inspired some to take up the cause,
Made Harrisburg & Washington
Pass clean air laws.

Denora, Denora, we weep for our dead.
"Clean air or a paycheck," is all that they said.
Denora, Denora, oh weep for your dead.
"Clean air or a paycheck," is all that they said.

So when you hear calls to abolish EPA
Remember Denora & those toxic smog days.
"Clean air or a paycheck," is all that they said.

Alien

747 on fire mid-air
Everyone could perish, but don't despair
'Cause in flies our hero, Superman
One breath, fire out, plane he lands.
(Bump, pa, bump-bump-bump, bump pa-bump)

Next day, big to-do, the Governor
To give Superman a medal for
Saving everyone on that plane
(Didn't know he did it for Lois Lane.)

Just at the big moment
Governor makes sudden movement
Clamps handcuffs with such zeal
Of Kryptonite, on the Man of Steel.

Glint in-his eye, Lex Luthor,
Just elected governor
On a platform, screw the poor
& Shove all immigrants out the door.

This is what he said, that Lex Luthor:
"Superman's an alien, Superman's an alien!
Superman's an alien, arrest him!
Superman's an alien, Superman's an alien!
Superman's an alien, deport him!"

Declares, "America is no place
For orphans of an alien race
& That cape & tights just scream queer."
At our hero, that crowd now jeers:

"Superman's an alien, Superman's an alien!
Superman's an alien, arrest him!
Superman's an alien, Superman's an alien!
Superman's an alien, deport him!"

They sent him home in a rocket ship,
Made damn sure it was a one-way trip.
Now an asteroid's heading straight for you
Superman's gone, so guess you're screwed.

Yeah, an asteroid's heading straight for us
Superman's gone, so guess we're fucked.

Take Root

A man standing at the bus stop
Between tokes gripes angrily
'bout immigrants stealing all the jobs
& Calls 'em damn lazy.
Sees a woman in a hijab sitting
& In her face he bawls,
"Go home, you terrorist! –
We're gonna build that wall!"
But his daughters are watching
And soon the youngest cries
'Cause sees that woman's suffering,
For hate too young or wise.

And which of these will take root:
The hatred or humanity?
Will the vine of bigotry wither,
Fade the fields of enmity?

At a florist in a nearby town
Two men order bouquets
For their upcoming wedding
But she refuses for they are gay.
Her teenage son who works there
Hears her words as said to him
For he knows he is different in ways
His mother condemns as sin.
Which path will he choose, I wonder,
Self-acceptance or disdain?
Declare as damned all men like him,
Or will love heal his pain?

For which of these will take root:
The hatred or humanity?
Will the vine of bigotry wither,
Fade the fields of enmity?

Her father praises leaders
Who believe they are kings
And so entitled to reach out
& Grab most anything.
But she, just turned thirteen,
Wonders what he means:
Does her dad think she exists
To fulfill such men's dreams?
And his little boy, what will he
Become when he's a man?
Now just wants to cheer up
His sister as best he can.

For which of these will take root:
The hatred or humanity?
Will the vine of bigotry wither,
Fade the fields of enmity?

Will our children harvest peace,
Discord no longer grow?
Or will their generation reap
These thistles we did sow?

For what you plant may take root:
What you feed, vitality.
May the vine of bigotry wither,
Fade the fields of enmity.

Hatred or Humanity –
Which one will it be?
Hatred or Humanity?

Hatred or Humanity –
Which one will we see?
Hatred or Humanity?

Christmas in the Airport

Were goin' to see Aunt Lucy, out there in LA,
Excited to see my cousins, looking forward to Christmas day.
Snow started falling as dad parked the car
First flight was bumpy, but we made it that far.
Alas, our luck sure changed, 'cause now it's so clear
We're celebrating Christmas in the airport this year.
Yeah, we're celebrating Christmas in the airport this year.

All socked in, not a single flight is goin' in or out
We're here for the long haul, of that we have no doubt.
Called every hotel, but no room for us in any inn,
Had to stake out a row of chairs to our chagrin.
As snow whips 'gainst the windows, driven by a mighty cold breeze,
We're resigned to a Christmas dinner of Five Guys & Chinese.
We're celebrating Christmas in the airport this year.

Watched videos 'til my batteries died,
       read a book 'til my eyes grew tired.
Could tell that dad was stewing on all that had transpired.
Went searching for some Coke & Nibs,
       like a quest for the Grail,
But vending machines depleted, even pretzels and ginger ale.
Bought the very last deck of cards, but soon bored of solitaire,
No one up for hearts or spades, all around me just despair.
Yes, we're celebrating Christmas in the airport this year.

In vain I stared at the snow outside and prayed that it would melt
While a toddler in mid-tantrum expressed what we all felt.
We were all protective of our luggage, of our space,
Who knew what danger might be lurking in each stranger's face?
Everyone settled in what little territory they could seize
Lights had dimmed, TVs offs, nothing festive, just unease.

When a clock struck midnight, 'twas a silent Christmas morn,
Then on cue a baby cried as if just born.
A guy leaned over & whispered to dad, who laughed at some joke,
Then mom offered 'em all cookies
      & for a moment the dark cloud broke.
They were from Albuquerque & were headed to Maine.
Their kid tossed me a chocolate coin, I gave her a candy cane.
A spirit of sharing began to spread out like a wave
Soon stories & jokes, food & drink everyone gave.
People made more room for others, no longer strangers,
Now people just like themselves, impromptu neighbors.

My sister starting singing, then stood upon her chair,
Rudolph the Red-Nosed Reindeer, her voice rang through the air.
One by one the rest of us – adults and kids – sang, too,
Hark the Herald, then Dreidel Dreidel, accompanied on kazoo.
"Let's go carol to the other gates," she said & off we went
Pakistani futball club by gate 19 joined in.
We're celebrating Christmas in the airport this year.

A kid headed to Miami blew up a beach ball
We had a wild soccer game, us kids big & small.
No bed, no shower, no change of clothes, no presents or a tree,
But even here among strangers, Christmas can come you see.
No one knows when we'll ever get out of here
But for this moment, with our new friends,
      we've found Christmas cheer.
We're celebrating Christmas in the airport this year.

Yeah, we're celebrating Christmas
In the airport this year.

Peace, Love & Tacos

We've forgotten to be wise
Failed to tell truth from lies
Now find ourselves so polarized &
Face what seem eternal gray skies.

Need sunrises & rainbows
And a few more hugs
And avocados (oh, yeah!)
For our taste buds.

Peace, Love & Tacos
Peace, Love & Tacos
Should be our new motto:
Peace, Love & Tacos.

Whether Chipotles or Moe's
Taco truck outside Lowe's
Local Tex-Mex bar & dive
Takeout eaten as you drive.

Chicken or steak, on either dine,
Fish or black bean, it's all fine.
Flour or masa, can't decide,
I'll go to Taco Heaven when I die.

Peace, Love & Tacos
Peace, Love & Tacos
With fresh tomato
Peace, Love & Tacos.

No matter how you did vote
We're all in the same boat
& It's hard to hate your fellow man
With a hearty taco in your hand.

& That woman you call an enemy?
Well, you just might find some empathy
As over tacos you both realize
A connection in each other's eyes.

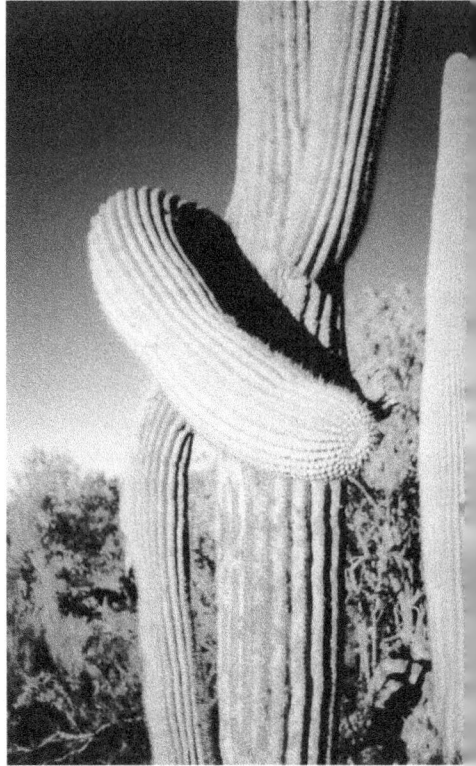

Peace, Love & Tacos
Peace, Love & Tacos
Es muy bueno!
Peace, Love & Tacos.

So welcome the immigrant & foreigner
& No more walls construct
For my dream, on every corner,
To find a taco truck.

& Also some falafel
Currywurst mit pommes
Woman selling gyros
& Baklava like her mom's.

Peace, Love & Tacos
Peace, Love & Tacos
We cry out bravo!
For Peace, Love & Tacos.

So let me treat you
To a taco heaped with guac
And if we part as friends
Why, it wouldn't be a shock.

Wash it down with Tecaté
(Negra Modelo if dark prefer)
Over beer & tacos, they say,
Miracles can occur.

Peace, Love & Tacos
Peace, Love & Tacos
Pax Mexicano!
Peace, Love & Tacos.

Peace, Love & Tacos
Peace, Love & Tacos
Yo quiero!
Peace, Love & Tacos
Ich will, je veux,
Peace, Love & Tacos.

Scale

"Damn!"
"Bloody hell!"
Look down in despair
At flesh that droops
& Hangs in ways
I wish would not.

My worth in one number
(The smaller the better),
Not down (yet again!)
Not even steady, but
Still creeping up –
Like ... entropy.

Scour my recall
Of the day before
As I self-flagellate:
Why that donut?
Why seconds at dinner?
Why not the treadmill?
Why the ice cream?

I vow to do better!
That my renewed
Self-control
Will ensure I succeed,
& Reach
My elusive goal.

But my mind's already at lunch
Sitting at Five Guys
With a bacon cheeseburger
& An order of fries.

Rebellion

Grocery shopping at Giant
hear The Clash
over the sound system
(*"Shareef don't like it ..."*)
and start singing along,
momentarily buoyed.

Then realized
in horror
that my youth's
music of Rebellion
has become
glorified
elevator music.

Pottery Shards

Bag of Worries Blues

Bag of worries, just dragging me down,
Bag of worries I'm always carrying around.
Dare not open it, dare not put it down.

There's a time bomb in there just tickin' away
Sure there's something vital in there due today.
I'll be free if only I could make it go away.

None were really that hard, but I left them far too long.
I should just do them now, but the repulsion is just too strong.
Instead I think I'll just sing you this song.

I promise I'll do the work soon, just keep waiting'.
In fact, I'll do the work over which I've been delayin'
As soon as I read all these books about not procrastinatin'.

Bag of worries, just dragging me down,
Bag of worries I'm always carrying around.
Dare not open it, dare not put it down.

Told to ponder my values and write a mission statement,
Put first things first, seek what's important.
I made lots of lists, everything labeled urgent.

I should just open that bag & see what's inside.
Why, "Open that bag & see what's inside"
Is action number one, but from it I can't help but hide.

I color-coded everything in single-file folders,
Organized my office supplies in a decorative holder,
But that bag of worries just began to smolder.

Bag of worries, just dragging me down,
Bag of worries I'm always carrying around.
Dare not open it, dare not put it down.

I just need to escape to where I won't feel so forlorn
Where the skies are blue, and no one care-worn.
Start afresh in a new life in a new town & be reborn.

Find some mystical girl there who'll give me shelter from this storm
She'd be spunky, quirky, and refuse to conform.
With her, I'd realize my dreams, my life transform.

But that's just an illusion, an adolescent fantasy,
Fed to us by Hollywood in many a movie.
I'd just start a new bag of worries 'cause the problem is me.

Bag of worries, just dragging me down,
Bag of worries I'm always carrying around.
Dare not open it, dare not put it down.

If some tragedy were to befall me, something fatal,
Why I'd never have to open it, it's just that simple.
No more stress over it, a solution tranquil.

Today's the date, time to drink from this cup.
Today's the date, I'll finally open it up,
But voices in my head say, "Just give up."

Let me first just quick check my email
Update my Facebook status, can't let it go stale,
And there's that video of a kitten chasing its tail
Corgi playing tetherball, I laugh without fail
& that Greg Klyma video about eating more kale
& that Greg Klyma video about how we should all
                              Eat More Kale.

Timeless Toy

When you hang me from your hand
See how all my coils expand.
Careful not to tangle me
Else may never get me free.
My spacey echo laser sounds
Psychedelic if you look down
Twist me & I will gyrate
When I'm dropped, I levitate.

Oscillating up & down; mesmerizing, I astound.
If you vibrate me just right, resonate with you I might.
As I slink & go down stairs, no one does it with more flair.

Simple harmonic oscillator
A physics educator
Harder you pull, the more I stretch –
Why, Hooke's Law is the best!
Omega squared = k over m
Send a pulse from end to end.
Stretch me out & pluck sideways
Watch me make some transverse waves.

Oscillating up & down; mesmerizing, I astound.
If you vibrate me just right, resonate with you I might.
As I slink & go down stairs, no one does it with more flair.

Richard James invented me
Back in the early 1940's
Working one day dropped a spring
& Saw it do an amazing thing.
His wife Betty coined my name
In Philly I first gained fame
When demonstrated how I play
& I sold out in just one day.

Oscillating up & down; mesmerizing, I astound.
If you vibrate me just right, resonate with you I might.
As I slink & go down stairs, no one does it with more flair.

One day, Richard, he found God
Left us all & went abroad
But Betty never lost her zeal
For a toy made of spring steel.
And she kept my cost low
So all kids could enjoy me so
A National Toy of the USA
Made right here in PA.
(Hollidaysburg, PA)

Oscillating up & down; mesmerizing, I astound.
If you vibrate me just right, resonate with you I might.
As I slink & go down stairs, no one does it with more flair.

A favorite at the science camp
Got my very own postage stamp
I'm metal, plastic, large & small,
Dog & train, worm & eyeballs.
In your hands, slosh me left-right
So relaxing, a delight!
Oh what joy can be found
In a coil that's helix wound.

Oh what joy in a timeless toy!
Oh what joy in a timeless toy!
Oh what joy in a timeless toy!
Oh what joy in a timeless – Pennsylvania – toy!

Just Let Me Sleep

Clock reads 6 am, dog's whining to go pee,
If I don't let him out soon, a puddle there'll be.
Get up in a daze, let him out in the yard,
Drop back in bed to hear him barking so hard.

Now the cats are meowing, banging on the door,
They're desperate for food, I can't take it no more.
But this bed is so soft, so cozy & warm,
Wish none of these cats had ever been born.

Chorus:
'Cause I just want to sleep, I just want to sleep,
For pity's sake, just let me sleep!
World, spin on ahead and leave me behind,
I'm worn to the bone, done in by the grind.
For once, can't you just let me sleep?
For pity's sake, God, just let me sleep.

Punk rocker son screeched guitar past midnight
Now my daughter's playing piano here at first light.
Construction next door, curse that circular saw,
Running it this early should be against the law.

Neighbor on the other side's now mowing his lawn
Only a nutcase like him would do it at dawn.
Sick of this noise, I want it no more!
Everyone, go away, leave me in silence galore.

Chorus

Will no one show this worn-out soul some mercy?
What sadist set the alarm clock this early?
That snooze button is just a nasty old tease.
A mere half hour, can't you give me that please?

Yes to sleep, perchance to dream, as Hamlet said.
Unlike Zevon, can't wait to sleep 'til I'm dead.
But my wife's listing off all her chores for me
That I need to sleep she can't seem to see.

Chorus

Come on dear, the world won't end
If another half hour in bed I spend.
Or even a whole hour, maybe even two,
Or three or four, yes that's what I'll do.
Five or six, seven or eight,
I'll stay here 'til dinner – yeah, that'll be great!
For pity's sake, God, just let me sleep …

Ain't Gonna Let It Break Me

Up at 5 am, train before school,
Classes over, it's back to the track.
Run for hours, then the ice pack.
A scout in the stands, scholarship on the line,
His big chance, runs his big race,
Trips halfway, falls on his face.
As he limped 'cross the finish line, a distant last place,
I heard him declare, of defeat not a trace:

Chorus:
Kicked in the gut, but I'll be back tomorrow,
Sucker punched, but I'll beat back the sorrow.
I ain't gonna let it break me, I ain't gonna let it take me
Down to those depths where I doubt my own worth
Paralyzed, bereft, sunk deep in the Earth.
Yeah, I ain't gonna let it shake me, I ain't gonna let it break me.

First gen student, bears her family's hopes,
Engineering major, bridges she'll build.
Each night waits tables to pay the bills.
Studied so hard for the first test
But sadly her score was a big blow
The class mean she was far below.
Her eyes watered as she left class,
But I heard her declare as she walked past:

Chorus

In the school play, on opening night,
First time cast in a leading role,
An acting career his ultimate goal.
His big speech in the pivotal scene
Knew it by heart, dreamed he'd shine,
But missed his cue, blanked on his line.
Flubbed it so bad, might have quit then & there,
But later that evening I heard him declare:

Chorus

Papers rejected, grant turned down,
Comments were brutal, reviewers were cruel,
Felt like I was back in the hell of high school.
Big research project, my life for five years,
All falling apart, worst day of my career.
Hard drive crashed to add to my cheer.
Wanted to quit, curl up in a ball,
Then recalled the words I'd heard from them all:

Chorus

Yeah, I ain't gonna let it shake me,
I ain't gonna let it break me.

Middle-Aged Rock Gods

When we were young, our guitar playing was cool,
Now our wives claim we're crazy, deluded old fools.
Girls thought us so hot in our skin-tight jeans;
Thirty years later we're busting the seams.

"Go play in the basement, out in the garage,"
Our wives & kids demand, they never applaud.
"How embarrassing," they say. "Go act your age!
Haven't you grown up yet? You're too old for this stage."

But as long as Jagger's out there, we will be, too.
Smoked less than Keith Richards, expect more than you.
We're middle-aged rock gods who get a bit soused,
Crank it up to 11 – and rock the house!

We can't play those slick licks like we did before,
Back when we had talent, hair, eyesight & more.
But we've got experience, we've lived more of life &
We've sure got the blues thanks to our ex-wives.

The Clash, The Jam, Pink Floyd, The Stones,
The Who, The Band, The Dead, the Ramones.
Yeah, we were around when the greatest bands played;
Neil Young said 'twas better to burn out than to fade.

But as long as Jagger's out there, we will be, too.
Smoked less than Keith Richards, expect more than you.
We're middle-aged rock gods who get a bit soused,
Crank it up to 11 – and rock the house!

We knew music as analog, not zeroes and ones,
As something you savored, not in a download comes.
We'd study the cover, caress the vinyl,
Our Zeppelin was Led & our Tap was Spinal.

Imperfect & real with no autotune,
Don't give a damn if you think us buffoons
'Cause our music is coming straight from the soul:
Like wine or whisky – it's better old.

'Cause as long as Jagger's out there, we will be, too.
Smoked less than Keith Richards, expect more than you.
We're middle-aged rock gods who get a bit soused,
Crank it up to 11 – and rock the house!

When we were young our guitar playing was cool,
Now they claim we're crazy deluded old fools.
But we're middle-aged rock gods who get a bit soused,
Crank it to up 11 – *and rock the house!*

Inspiration

When inspiration comes
      You need to act then.
Think, "I'll remember it later,"
      But you never do when
You recall that you'd had
      A visit from the Muse,
But as hard as you strain
      That thought you did lose.

Get it down now,
      Don't ever wait,
Even a momentary delay
      May be too late.
Else someone distracts you
      Alas, for too long
With their problems or asking,
      "Are you writing a song?"

Inversely proportional
      Inspiration comes round
To your ability that moment
      To write it down.
Most come ill-formed,
      Rarely complete,
While driving, mid-shower,
      Or drifting to sleep.

They press to burst forth,
      When you least have the time
When the work's piled high
      When you face a deadline.
But that important project?
      You'll forget even its name
And that gift of creation
      You'll be glad you did claim.

It's Your Fault, You Know

Lost out here, GPS dead.
A shortcut, yes that's what I'd said.
"As always, a fiasco," you finally exclaim.
Well if you knew better, then you're partly to blame.
'Cause you should have stopped me, you should have said no.
You didn't put your foot down, so it's your fault, you know.

Deep frying the turkey, bragged I was a pro,
But quickly became a giant fiery inferno.
Said you knew it would happen, said it with a laugh,
Well, then, of the blame you should claim half.
'Cause you should have stopped me, you should have said no.
You didn't put your foot down, so it's your fault, you know.

Now water's squirting all over the new wooden floor.
You complained the faucet leaked, so don't get so sore.
To repair it, I tried, don't need your blame dance.
You could have called the plumber when you had the chance.
'Cause you should have stopped me, you should have said no.
You didn't put your foot down, so it's your fault, you know.

On your keyboard, a freshly killed mouse.
Peaches looks proud, yet you only grouse.
You're partly to blame, so don't get mad at me,
You never should have let me get that cat you see.
'Cause you should have stopped me, you should have said no.
You didn't put your foot down, so it's your fault, you know.

My boss' latest scheme, a disaster I could see.
I begged, I pleaded, but he wouldn't listen to me.
Now that it's imploded, all gone pear-shaped,
I deal with the fallout while the blame he escapes.
Yeah, he said …
"You should have seen it coming, spoken up, said no.
It's your department, so it's your fault, you know."

Our son skateboarded down Suicide Hill,
Broke his wrist, nearly got himself killed.
Turned to me as he was getting his cast,
"You never should have let me try to go that fast.
'Cause you should have stopped me, you should have said no.
You didn't put your foot down, so it's your fault, you know."

Go to answer the door, dog stole my steak,
Left it for a moment, he was quick as a snake.
On our white living room carpet he gobbled it down,
Looks at me all guiltless amid patches of brown.
(Showed no remorse for his transgression,
I could read his expression… which clearly said:)
"Yes, you left it out, a gift you bestowed,
You could have stood guard, so it's your fault, you know."

Looking around, I can see you hate this song,
You think it's dreadful & you might not be wrong.
But if my lyrics and singing bring tears to your ears,
Well, you chose to stay & not walk out of here.
You should have seen it coming, spoken up, said no.
You gave me the microphone, so it's your fault, you know.

Sword Form

for Amalia Shaltiel

My body knows it
My muscles remember
1000 forms &
A half dozen years.

But this spring
With sword in hand,
After its winter-long absence,
My mind gets in the way
As it demands to plan
The next move or two
& Critiques,
"You sure screwed up,"
Or, "So far so good."

But the less my mind
Attempts recall,
The more I can listen
To how my sword speaks;
The more I release,
The more I feel its flow,
For now an exercise
In letting go.

Marie Kondo Blues

Going through our stuff,
One by one,
Piece by piece,
As Marie Kondo's
KonMari Method
We endeavor
To employ.
Holding each item up,
Asking,
"Does this
Spark joy?"

But after the umpteenth time,
I exclaim,
"Oh, screw this!
I mean, really,
Isn't that too much to ask?"
I say to my wife.
"For each sock, each pair
Each single underwear,
To provide sparkle
& Meaning to my life?"

"Let's keep it all," I say.
"And in the future someday,
Our kids can go through it
After we pass away."

Jigsaw Puzzle

Today we are introducing
An exciting new service,
An innovative
Out-of-the-box
Approach
For downloading
The latest hit movies
& Paparazzi starlet photos.

For a nominal fee
(Of course),
We'll send you all the
0's and 1's
Already sorted
(First the 0s,
Then the 1s)
And all you need to do
To see
Your photo
Or movie   1001000100
Is put them   1010011010
In   0010100110
Order.   0011010101
                            0101001101

Plectra Perplexion

for Jon Vickers-Jones

The question that perplexes me
Is this:
Do guitar picks
End up in the same place
As socks?

While a single sock
May disappear from each laundry load,
Half the picks I bring to a gig or open mike
Never make it back home.

I imagine tiny Arrietty secretly
Stashing them,
    In a cache
    Of green
      Star-holed
      Plectra
& Her fellow Borrowers having some vital need of
    Gray nylon rounded triangles
      Coarse-gridded for friction.

Or perhaps my green & gray picks
    Just annihilate each other
    Like positrons & electrons,
      Their quantum wavefunctions
      Destructively interfering.

Or, just maybe,
    Like Jon's Gypsy sock,
    They yearn to see the world,
      And so hit the road
      To live the life
        Their owner
        Only dreams of.

The Taco Truck

Going to the Taco Truck, Taco Truck, Taco Truck
Going to the Taco Truck down on Locust Lane.

El Gringo's where I eat lunch, I eat lunch, I eat lunch
El Gringo's where I eat lunch, Tuesdays sun or rain.

Ben & Greg make it fresh, make it fresh, make it fresh.
Masa dough they make it fresh, how it tastes so fine.

Avocadoes they do mash, they do mash, they do mash
Watch them avocadoes mash for their guac divine.

So let's go to the Taco Truck, Taco Truck, Taco Truck,
Meet me at the Taco Truck, with one bite you'll be hooked.

What's in the tamales, tamales, tamales?
Chicken, pork or zucchini? In corn husks they've been cooked.

I hope they have my favorite drink, favorite drink, favorite drink.
Watermelon's the best I think, but sure love ginger lime!

I hear the tacos are b-lack bean b-lack bean, b-lack bean,
I hear the tacos are b-lack bean, with goat cheese they're sublime.

So join me at the Taco Truck, Taco Truck, Taco Truck,
A short line so we're in luck. At the Taco Truck.
Yeah, love that Taco Truck!

Lies in Sleep

The lies that seep into our minds
In the middle of the night
Come to bring only harm,
To accuse, to suspect,
To reawaken old grievances
To freshly inflict the pain
And amplify the hurt
In sleepless dark hours.

These thoughts wish us ill,
Though why I don't know.
'Twas such thoughts that led
To Macbeth's & Othello's demise.
Such thoughts are ignored,
Put aside, by those wise.
For the world is at its bleakest,
These hours when all terrible
Things can be believed
And all contradicting evidence
(or even basic common sense)
Seem hard to find.

So when those thoughts grab you
& Pull you from sleep,
Don't let them stew in your head,
Grow like a disease.
Just put 'em aside &
Go back to your dreams,
Else write them down so later
You can laugh at them
Come morning
In the sun's beams.

You Poemed

You poemed.
I didn't.
You tweeted.
I didn't.
Not that we don't care,
But once in a while,
Keep it to yourself.
Please.

Fellow Tourist

A phallic extension
So your face can block the view
I came to appreciate beauty
& Prefer to see it without you.

I am too humble to believe
That my visage could enhance
What I had traveled so far
To experience this one chance.

And what's more, you don't
Even seem to look!
To soak in what's behind you
In that photo you just took.

I'm really quite a gentle dude
Not to violence am I prone,
But I'd like to snap that "selfie stick"
And off the cliff toss your phone.

They Told Me

They told me that Muslims
Were the threat of the day
So I voted for those
Who'd send them away.
Though my paycheck's still shrinking
& I've got no health care,
I've still got my guns
& We've brought back school prayer.

Question Not Asked

A man staggered erratically crossing the street
And we waited & waited for him to get out of our way.

"How many points for hitting him?" I almost asked you,
But we sat in silence 'til he finally passed,
Unharmed, by us, at least.

"I know that guy," you then piped up,
Adding "I really can't stand him!"

"Good thing I never asked, then,"
I mused,
As we drove away.

The Ant

An ant is clearly stalking me
First in the kitchen, which I understood,
Next on the dining room table,
Near some tasty home-baked goods.

But then it's on my keyboard
In my office where there's no food.
Then worse, in our bedroom,
Where it really killed the mood.

It's on the toilet paper roll
On my leg, my reading chair.
Just when I think he's finally left
I find him crawling there.

As I go to jot down a lyric
Of beauty that's come to mind
And right there on my notebook
That damn ant again I find.
And in my startled frame of mind
I'd lost that exquisite line,
My only chance with it gone,
Of my future, a bad sign.

Yes, that this ant is stalking me,
All I can count on from now on,
& Everywhere I go I'll see
This *Formicidae* demon spawn.

Vienna Driver (*Wiener Fahrer*)

Dear Vienna driver:
Was it really necessary
To honk your horn
So loudly,
Not to mention several times?
For there's barely any traffic
Now, a quarter to midnight,
And since it's yet another scorcher
Everyone's windows are wide open
So your momentary annoyance
Affected *fünfzehn* (50) or so of us
Startled from our slumbers
And in our sleepy heads
Cursing you the fuck out.

Good-bye Washer

You've scrubbed clean
    our underwear
        & dirty socks
    for 13 years.

But you won't start.
    Been sad to hear
        you falling apart,
    stripping your gears.

The time to replace
    & not repair
        has finally come;
    yes, one can tell.

We release you now
    to rest in peace
        in Silicon Heaven[*],
    where you will dwell.

Your friend who's always
    stood by you there
        will remain with us
    to dry our tears.

So good-bye washer,
    you've served us well.

[*] from the television show *Red Dwarf*

Silence

Boldly
I called out to the world,
But the world answered not.
A crushing silence
My only reply.

So instead
I sang it a song,
Hauntingly beautiful,
But again just silence,
No other reply.

The next day I tried once more
Called out, "World! I am here!"
& Sang it another song –
But a little less bold,
A little less beautiful,
Than I had dared
The day before.

Again only silence
Again no reply.

Each day, I did this
Until my voice itself nearly silent,
My song a mere whispered despair,
Until even I myself
Could hear it no more.

And still no reply.

Photographs

Unless stated otherwise, photographs were taken by the author.
Cover: Asbury Park, New Jersey, boardwalk & Casino arcade shell
i. Train tracks in Zell am See, Austria
iii. Gondola tower on the Schmittenhöche in the Austrian Alps
vi. Wiener Riesenrad in the Prater (Vienna, Austria)
1. Covered pedestrian bridge in Rothenburg ob der Tauber, Germany
2. Sleeping Bear Dunes National Lakeshore (Michigan)
5. Stereogram images of Penn State's campus
7. Sunrise over Bradley Beach, New Jersey
8. Boardwalk in Ocean Grove, New Jersey
9. Interior of the Casino arcade shell in Asbury Park, New Jersey
10. Muir Woods National Monument in Marin County, California
11. Brooklyn Bridge, New York City
12. San Francisco Cable Car
13. Johnstown Incline (Pennsylvania)
16. Backstage at the Halbritter Center at Juniata College (Pennsylvania)
18. Tulips in bloom on Penn State's campus
19. Marilyn Meyers & Jay Van Hook on Dutch Man in playground in
    Orange City, Iowa, in 1975. Photograph taken by Mary Van Hook.
20. Cows along the Großglockner Hochalpenstraße in Austria
23. Windmill Bank in Orange City, Iowa, in 1975. Photograph taken by
    Mary Van Hook.
28. Petřín Tower in Prague, Czech Republic
32. Shadows in Osmond Laboratory, Penn State University
35. Prague Castle, Czech Republic
36. Spiral staircase to pulpit at Stephansdom in Vienna, Austria
37. Base of pulpit in Stephansdom in Vienna, Austria
40. Tree in Yosemite National Park in California
43. Ocean Grove, New Jersey, meeting house cross lit up at night

44. Statue of Jesus in Stephansdom in Vienna, Austria.

49. Victoria Falls in Zimbabwe

52. Pier in Ocean Grove, New Jersey, (upper) before and (lower) several years after Hurricane Sandy hammered the Jersey shore

53. Water tower under construction on the Penn State campus

57. Empress Elisabeth (Sisi) of Austria on a sign in Zell am See, Austria, about Sisi's hiking up the Schmittenhöhe on August 9, 1885

59. Statue of Austrian Kaiser & King of Hungary Franz Joseph in the Burggarten in Vienna, Austria

62. Candle and its reflections at Winterpark Presbyterian Church (Florida)

63. Reflection of lamp in front & rear surfaces of a magnifying glass

65. Bust of Dietrich Bonhoeffer in a chapel at the Flossenbürg Concentration Camp, Germany

67. Statue of Liberty

71. A foggy day in Salzburg, Austria

72. Former Nazi parade grounds outside Nuremberg, Germany

78. Saguaro National Park outside Tucson, Arizona

79. Taco truck design created by Dietre Van Hook for the cover of my 2017 album *Peace, Love & Tacos*

79. Chairs & reflective table in Chipotles (State College, Pennsylvania)

81. St. Alkmund's Church in Shrewsbury, England

83. Petřín Tower in Prague, Czech Republic

86. London Eye (England)

87. Trebuchet at Warwick Castle in England

90. Garden in park in north Berkeley, California

93. The Great Zimbabwe

94. Jim Colbert & Stephen Van Hook playing at the Granary in Lemont, Pennsylvania. Photograph taken by Jon Vickers-Jones.

96. Church ruin in Bacharach, Germany

99. Arthur's Seat in Edinburgh, Scotland

100. Amalia Shaltiel and Evan Foster engaged in Tai Chi swordplay

102. Equipotential diagram created for physics class

104. Elevator shaft in Prague town hall (Czech Republic)

107. Ben Stanley, proprietor of the El Gringo taco truck, at a farmer's market in State College, Pennsylvania

108. Block & table in Hohenwerfen Castle in Austria

110. Sculpture in Prague Castle (Czech Republic)

111. Face inside south tower of Stephansdom in Vienna, Austria

113. The Belvedere Museum in Vienna, Austria

114. Deutsches Historisches Museum in Berlin, Germany

117. Japanese Garden in late winter in Meijer Gardens (Michigan)

119. View of Stephansplatz from Stephansdom's south tower (Vienna)

120. Half Dome at Yosemite National Park in California

122. Asbury Park, New Jersey, Casino arcade shell (Ocean Grove side)

Notes

Lyrics referenced in "Fellow Christian" are from the popular Christian hymn *They'll Know We Are Christians* by Peter Scholtes (1966).

Lyrics referenced in "Rebellion" are from *Rock the Casbah* by The Clash on their 1982 album *Combat Rock*.

"House of Sinners & Saints" borrows elements from many sources, including the Bible (Joseph from Genesis), Tony Campolo (the prostitute & the cake), Dietrich Bonhoeffer's *The Cost of Discipleship*, Victor Hugo's *Les Miserables*, and Saint Augustine's *Confessions*.

"Mark of Cain" was inspired by Michelle Alexander's powerful essay *Incarceration Nation* broadcast on Alternative Radio (2012).

"Three Drams, Four" was inspired by Compton Mackenzie's *Whisky Galore* and Roger Hutchinson's *Polly: The True Story Behind Whisky Galore*.

"Refugee" was written on January 28, 2017, as Donald Trump's Executive Order travel ban was wreaking havoc on people's lives.

Thanks to Chuck Adams & Mark McCarthy for sharing some of their recollections about high school with me for "Facing Walls".

"If You Only Played Guitar" was inspired in part by the show *Red Dwarf*.

www.ingramcontent.com/pod-product-compliance
Lightning Source LLC
Chambersburg PA
CBHW032007040426
42448CB00006B/512